Caribbean Vegan Recipes

*30+ Tasty and Healthy Curated Recipes To
Impress and Enjoy*

Introduction

Did you that the Caribbean consists of a collection of over 7,000 islands, 13 countries and a dozen or so territories around the southeast of Florida and northeast of South America? Needless to say, it's a diverse set of island nations, and each island is unique.

Caribbean food is known as a type of "fusion" cuisine and its flavors are full of energy and flavor. It truly is a melting pot of various cultures from African, Asian, and possibly even European.

In recent years, veganism has been gaining in popularity as well. People have decided to go vegan for various reasons, including health and ethical ones. In fact, research after research has shown that veganism can help promote weight loss, reduce risk of heart disease, and even help lower risk of certain cancers.

The goal of this Caribbean Vegan cookbook is to provide you with a curated collection of tasty and fun-to-make recipes that will not only satisfy your own cravings and bring you enjoyment, but impress your family and friends as well.

This cookbook brings together the best of both worlds — that is, Caribbean flavors that are accommodating to individuals following veganism.

A diverse and eclectic set of recipes are included in this cookbook including black rum cake, vegan curry, black bean mango wraps (just to name a few), and more.

Cornmeal

Ingredients

- 1 cup cornmeal (fine)
- 1 cup water
- 2 cups almond milk
- 1/4 teaspoon cinnamon
- 1 cup coconut milk
- 1/3-1/2 cup pure cane sugar, or maple syrup
- 1 teaspoon vanilla
- 1/4 teaspoon nutmeg
- 1/3 teaspoon salt
- Banana slices
- Mango slices
- Passion fruit
- Toasted coconut flakes

Instructions

- Mix cornmeal in a medium bowl with water until it's smooth
- Bring almond milk, coconut milk and salt to bowl in a pot on medium-high heat.
- Add cornmeal mixture and stir continuously using a whisk. While the porridge thickens, it is important to continue mixing to prevent lumps from forming.

- Reduce heat and cover pot and allow porridge to simmer for about 10 minutes. Stir occasionally.
- Add sugar, vanilla, nutmeg, and cinnamon and allow cornmeal porridge to cook for 5 more minutes. Stir occasionally.
- Divide cornmeal porridge into 2 bowls, top with fruits and toasted coconut flakes.

Bean Soup and Greens

Ingredients

- 1 tablespoon coconut oil
- 1 onion, diced
- 3 garlic cloves, minced
- 1 teaspoon allspice
- 2 teaspoons freshly grated ginger
- 1-2 habanero or Scotch bonnet peppers, minced
- 1 teaspoon dried thyme
- 1/2 teaspoon ground cinnamon
- 1/2 teaspoon black pepper
- 2 cups vegetable broth
- 1 (14 ounce) can light coconut milk
- 1 (14 ounce) can fire roasted tomatoes
- 2 (14 ounce) cans red kidney beans, drained and rinsed
- 1 (14 ounce) can black beans, drained and rinsed
- 2 tablespoons lime juice
- 1 1/2 tablespoons organic brown sugar
- 1 medium bunch of collard greens (about 1 pound), stems removed and torn into 1-2 inch pieces
- Salt

Instructions

- Melt the coconut oil in a large pot over medium heat.
- Give the oil a minute or two to heat up, then add the onion.
- Cook the onion for about 5 minutes, stirring occasionally, until it becomes soft and translucent.
- Add the garlic, ginger, and habanero or Scotch bonnet pepper, continue to cook for about 1 minute, until fragrant.
- Stir in the allspice, thyme, cinnamon and black pepper, and cook for a few seconds, then stir in the broth, coconut milk, tomatoes, red beans, and black beans.
- Increase the heat and bring everything to a boil.
- Lower the heat and allow it to simmer, uncovered, for 10 minutes, until the beans soften up a bit.
- At this point you can optionally blend a small amount of the soup with an immersion blender or a conventional blender, if you'd like it to be thicker.
- Stir in the collard greens..
- Allow the soup to continue simmering for about 20 minutes, until the greens are soft and wilted.
- Remove the pot from heat and stir in the lime juice and brown sugar. Season with salt to taste.
- Serve.

Black Bean Mango Wraps

Ingredients

Jamaican Jerk Jackfruit:

- 20 oz (566 g) can young green jack fruit
- 2 tsp oil divided
- 1.5 tsp garlic powder
- 1 tsp onion powder
- 1 tsp thyme
- 1 tsp parsley
- 1/2 tsp (0.5 tsp) salt
- 1 tsp paprika
- 1/2 to 3/4 tsp cayenne
- 1/4 to 1/2 tsp black pepper
- a good dash of cinnamon, nutmeg and all spice.
- 1 tsp or more lime juice
- 2 cups (500 ml) water
- 1/4 to 1/2 tsp sugar or other sweetener

Caribbean Black Beans:

- 1 tsp oil
- 1/2 cup (80 g) chopped onion
- 2 cloves of garlic finely chopped

- 1 15 oz (425 g) can black beans or 1.5 cups cooked
- 1/4 tsp (0.25 tsp) all spice
- 1/2 tsp (0.5 tsp) thyme
- 1/4 tsp (0.25 tsp) cayenne
- 1/2 tsp (0.5 tsp) salt or to taste, depends on the beans
- 1.5 tbsp orange juice or 2 tsp lemon juice + 1/4 tsp sugar
- 1/4 cup (62.5 ml) water

Other additions:

- Chopped mango
- sliced cucumbers or pickles
- cilantro or baby greens
- salt pepper, lemon or lime juice
- large tortilla wraps

Instructions

Jamaican jerk Jackfruit:

- Drain the jackfruit and wash well.
- Squeeze out the liquid really well by pressing the jackfruit pieces in a paper napkin. Shred in a food processor or thinly slice using a knife. (For more flavor, toss the shredded jackfruit in the spices, herbs, lime juice and marinate in the fridge for an hour or overnight. then cook with water)
- Heat 1 tsp oil in a skillet over medium heat. Add shredded jackfruit and all dry spices (or 1.5 tbsp or more premade jamaican jerk seasoning)
- Cook for 2-3 mins or until the spices start to smell roasted.

- Add lime juice and water and sugar and cook partially covered for 25 to 30 minutes. Stir occasionally.
- Once the mixture is dry, taste and adjust salt and heat. Add in the 1 tsp oil and continue to roast the jackfruit until golden brown on some edges. Serve this in wraps, sandwiches, tacos, nachos.

Make the Caribbean black beans:

- Heat oil in a skillet over medium heat. Add onions and garlic and cook until translucent. 4-5 mins.
- Add black beans, spices, water and orange or lime juice and simmer for 10 mins. Stir occasionally.

Make the wraps:

- Layer the black beans, then cilantro or chopped baby green, then a good helping of the jerk jackfruit, then cucumber and mango, lemon, salt and pepper. Fold into a burrito and serve.

Caribbean "Salt Fish"

Ingredients

- 820g heat of palms (2 cans)
- 2 spring onions
- 1 yellow onion
- 2 medium tomatoes
- 4 gloves garlic
- 1 red pepper
- 1 orange pepper
- 2 tbsp nori flakes
- 1 tsp fresh thyme
- juice of lemon
- pink salt and pepper
- handful of fresh parsley
- vegetable oil or water for cooking

Instructions

- Chop or pulse the heart of palm in a food processor until you get the right consistency.
- Chop the peppers and green onion and finely slice the yellow onion.
- Add the peppers and both onions in a pan and sauté for 5 minutes
- Add the remaining ingredients minus the parsley to the pan, mix well and cook for another 5 minutes.

- Turn off the heat then garnish with lots of fresh parsley.

Corn Fritters

Ingredients

For the fritters

- 1 quart of oil
- 3/4 cup all-purpose flour
- 1 flax egg
- ½ cup unsweetened non-dairy milk
- Salt, pepper, garlic powder to taste
- Cayenne Pepper
- 1 cup frozen or fresh sweet corn kernels
- ½ medium white onion, chopped
- ½ green pepper, chopped

For the dipping sauce

- 1 tbsp vegan mayonnaise
- 2 tbsp ketchup
- Salt and pepper to taste
- Juice of half a lime
- Half a tsp to one tsp of hot pepper sauce or hot sauce

Instructions

- Prepare flax egg by mixing one tbsp of ground flax seeds with three tbsp water. Set aside for 10 minutes.
- Mix dipping sauce ingredients together then set aside.
- Heat oil in pot or a deep fryer.
- In a medium bowl, combine flour and spices, mix together.
- Add milk, flax egg and crushed seaweed sheets, if using. Mix together.
- Drop batter into hot oil, one rounded tablespoon at a time.
- Fry fritters until golden brown. Remove from oil with a slotted spoon and drain on paper towels.

Plantain Lasagna

Ingredients

Filling

- 1/2 cup red or green lentils
- 2 cups water
- 1 tbsp cooking oil
- 1 onion, diced
- 2 cloves garlic, minced
- 7–8 mushrooms, diced
- 1/2 red bell pepper, diced
- 1/2 cup walnuts, crushed
- 1 tsp oregano
- 1/2 tsp cumin
- 1/4 tsp chili powder
- 1 14.5-ounce can diced tomatoes
- 2 tbsp tomato paste
- 1 tbsp apple cider vinegar
- 1/2 tsp salt

Plantains

- 4 ripe plantains
- 1/4 cup oil for frying

Cheese Sauce

- 1 and 1/2 cup almond milk
- 2 tbsp cornstarch
- 1 tbsp yeast
- 4 tbsp white miso
- 1 tsp white vinegar
- 1/2 tsp onion powder
- 1/4 tsp garlic powder
- 1/4 tsp salt

Instructions

Filling

- Rinse the lentils and place them in a saucepan. Add the water and bring to a boil. Once boiling, reduce the heat and let simmer for about 15 minutes, or until lentils are tender. Drain excess water if needed. Set the cooked lentils aside.
- Heat the tablespoon of oil in a large skillet over medium heat. Once hot, add the onion and garlic and cook for 3-5 minutes.
- Add the mushrooms and red bell pepper, and cook for another 7-10 minutes or until red bell peppers are soft.
- Add the cooked red lentils, slightly crushed walnuts, oregano, cumin, chili powder, diced tomatoes, tomato paste, apple cider vinegar, and salt.

- Cook for about 5-8 minutes over medium heat, stirring regularly. Taste and adjust seasonings if needed. Remove from heat and set aside while you prepare the bananas.

Plaintains

- Preheat oven to 350°F (180°C).
- Carefully peel the plantain, trying not to break them. Slice the plantains length-wise into thin strips
- Heat the oil in a large frying pan. Once hot, arrange the plantain slices in a single layer and fry for about 2-3 minutes per side, or until golden brown. Transfer to a plate with paper towel to drain excess oil. Repeat with the remaining plantain slices.
- Arrange a layer of plantain in a rectangular baking dish. Top with half of the filling. Repeat with another layer of plantains and the remaining filling.
- Prepare the cheese sauce: In a large saucepan, combine all the ingredients together and whisk well until the cornstarch is dissolved. Heat over medium heat, whisking regularly until it starts to boil. Once the sauce has thickened, remove from heat and pour over the filling in the baking dish.
- Top with one last layer of plantains and bake uncovered for 25-30 minutes. Let cool a few minutes.

- Leftovers will keep for up to 3 days in the refrigerator. To reheat, cover with aluminum foil and bake in a 350°F preheated oven for 30-40 minutes.

Caribbean Style Pasta

Ingredients

Walnut Balls

- 3 tablespoons coconut oil, for sautéing
- 2 cups chopped button mushrooms
- 2 small onions, sliced
- 1 cup walnut halves, soaked in 3 cups of water for at least 30 minutes
- 5 garlic cloves crushed
- 3 dates, pitted
- 3 tablespoons nutritional yeast
- 1 tablespoon Bragg Liquid Aminos
- 1 tablespoon fresh thyme leaves
- 1 tablespoon flax meal, soaked in 2 tablespoons of hot water for 3 minutes
- 1 tablespoon curry powder
- 1 tablespoon smoked paprika
- 1 teaspoon black pepper
- ¼ cup oat flour, plus 2 Tablespoons
- ¼ cup fine bread crumbs
- 2 tablespoons Jamaican Jerk Seasoning
- 2 teaspoons seasoning salt
- 1/2 cup neutral oil, for frying

Sauce

- 1 tablespoon coconut oil
- 1 tablespoon Madras curry powder, (or Thai curry powder, any color)
- 1 can coconut milk, (13.5 ounces)
- 1 small onion, diced
- 2 garlic cloves, pressed
- 1 tablespoon tamari, (or Bragg Liquid Aminos or soy sauce)
- 1 tablespoon chopped cilantro
- 1 teaspoon ground allspice
- 1 teaspoon sugar
- 1 teaspoon onion powder
- salt, to taste

Pasta

- 4 tablespoons olive or coconut oil, for sautéing
- 1/2 red bell pepper, thinly sliced
- 1/2 yellow bell pepper, thinly sliced
- 1/2 green bell pepper, thinly sliced
- 1 pound linguini, cooked al dente according to package directions

Instructions

- To make the walnut balls, heat the oil in a medium skillet over medium heat. Add the mushrooms and onions and sauté until the onions are translucent, about 5 minutes.

- Transfer the mixture to a food processor. Add the drained walnuts, garlic, dates, nutritional yeast, liquid aminos, thyme, flax meal mixed with hot water, curry powder, smoked paprika, and black pepper. Pulse until the nuts have been chopped fine but you still have texture.
- Transfer the mixture to a medium bowl and add the oat flour, bread crumbs, jerk seasoning, and seasoning salt. Form the mixture into twenty 1.5-inch balls.
- Preheat the oven to 350F and line a baking sheet with a silicone mat or parchment paper.
- Heat the neutral oil in a medium skillet over medium-high heat. Fry the walnut balls, until a thin brown crust is formed, 5 minutes.
- Transfer the balls to the baking sheet and bake for 20 minutes, or until the form an outer brown crust.
- Meanwhile, make the sauce. Heat the oil in a medium-sized pot heat. Add the curry and heat through, about 1 minute. Add the coconut milk, onion, garlic, soy sauce, cilantro, allspice, sugar, and onion powder and stir to combine. Taste and adjust for salt. Bring to a boil and stir until the mixture is fairly creamy.
- To finish the pasta, heat olive oil in a wok over high heat. Sauté the bell peppers until slightly tender, about 2 minutes. Add the pasta and heat through, tossing to combine, about 4 minutes. Add the sauce, to taste, and top with the walnut balls.
- To serve, layer the balls over pasta and top off with sauce.

Black Bean Sandwiches

Ingredients

Arepas

- 6 large arepas (or you could sub corn tortillas)

Plantains

- 2 large ripe and spotty plantains, peeled
- 1 Tbsp oil (avocado is my preferred)

Black Beans

- 1 15-ounce can black beans, slightly drained
- 1/2 tsp ground cumin
- 1 Pinch sea salt

Guacamole

- 2 ripe avocados
- 2-3 Tbsp lime juice
- 1/4 tsp sea salt (plus more to taste)

- 1/4 cup diced onion
- 2 Tbsp chopped cilantro

For Serving (optional)

- Cabbage
- Cilantro
- Habanero Hot Sauce (or other hot sauce)

Instructions

- If you haven't already prepared your arepas, which take about 30 minutes (not included in prep time), do that now.
- Preheat oven to 400 degrees F (209 C). Peel your plantains and slice on a diagonal into 1/2-inch pieces. Then add to a parchment-lined baking sheet and toss with oil. Arrange into an even layer and bake for about 15-20 minutes or until golden brown and caramelized. Toss near the 10-minute point to ensure even baking.
- In the meantime, add (slightly drained) black beans to a small saucepan and heat over medium heat until bubbly and hot. Season with cumin and salt and stir to combine. Then turn heat off and set aside (cover to keep warm).
- Lastly, prepare guacamole by mashing avocado in a small mixing bowl and adding lime, salt, onion, and cilantro.
- Stir to combine, and taste and adjust flavor as needed. Add more salt for saltiness, lime for acidity, or onion for crunch. Set aside.

Jerk Tofu with Pineapple Salsa

Ingredients

- 7-oz package extra firm tofu sliced into 8 planks and pressed
- 1/4 c jerk seasoning

Pineapple Salsa

- 2 c fresh pineapple, cored and diced
- 1 mango, diced
- 1 red bell pepper, diced
- 1 jalapeno, minced
- 1/4 c red onion, minced
- 1/4 c cilantro, chopped
- Juice of 1 lime

Instructions

- Combine salsa ingredients in a medium bowl and set aside.
- Rub the pressed tofu with jerk seasoning.
- Heat the grill to high heat and grill until tofu is warmed through and grill marks appear, about 2-4 minutes per side.

Velvety Herbed Pumpkin

Ingredients

- About 3 cups of pumpkin , skin removed and flesh cut roughly into 1/2-inch cubes

- 1 medium onion , finely chopped

- 3 cloves of garlic , minced

- 2 serrano or jalapeno chillies , finely chopped (use less if you like less heat, or take out the seeds and ribs)

- 7-8 medium-sized sage leaves , minced

- 2 tbsp finely chopped cilantro or coriander leaves

- 2 tsp sugar

- 1 tbsp canola or other vegetable oil

- Salt to taste

Instructions

- Heat the oil in a saucepan. Add the onions and stir-fry until they just start to brown.
- Add the garlic, chillies, sage and cilantro and stir for a few seconds. Now add the pumpkin cubes.
- Add 1/4 cup of water or vegetable stock and when the water begins to simmer, turn the heat to low, cover the saucepan, and let the pumpkin cook, stirring occasionally, for about 45 minutes or until it is buttery-soft and tender. Mash some of the pumpkins, if you like, for more texture.
- Add salt and sugar and turn off the heat.
- Serve hot with rotis

Vegan Spinach Soup

Ingredients

- Coconut Oil
- Onion
- Garlic
- Green Onion
- Celery
- Thyme
- Spinach
- Vegetable Bouillon
- Coconut Milk
- Vegetable Broth
- Allspice
- Scotch Bonnet Pepper
- Potato
- Dumpling (optional)

Instructions

- Heat oil in a large pot on medium heat, add onion and cook until soft, about 2 minutes. Stir in garlic, green onions, celery, thyme and cook until fragrant.
- Add spinach and stir until wilted. Add vegetable bouillon, coconut milk, vegetable broth, allspice berries, potatoes, dumplings, and Scotch Bonnet. Bring to a boil, reduce heat to simmer for about 25-30 minutes.

- For the dumplings: Place flour and salt in a bowl. Add water and mix to make a stiff dough. Pinch off small pieces of dough and roll into the palm of hands to make long thin dumplings. Drop into the simmering stew.

Instapot Vegan Potato Curry

Ingredients

- 2 tablespoons coconut oil
- 2 tablespoons curry powder
- 1 teaspoon paprika
- 1 teaspoon cumin
- 1 teaspoon turmeric powder
- 2 sprigs fresh thyme, or 1 teaspoon dried
- 1 cup onion, finely chopped
- 4 cloves garlic, mince
- 1 teaspoon fresh ginger, grated
- 2 green onions, chopped
- 20 ounce can green jackfruit, drained and rinsed
- 4 medium potatoes, cubed
- 1 medium carrot, diced
- 15 ounce can coconut milk
- 2 cups vegetable broth, or 2 cubes vegetable bouillon plus water
- 1 teaspoon Italian seasoning
- 1/4 -1/2 teaspoon Cayenne pepper, or 1 whole Scotch Bonnet pepper
- 1 batch dumpling (optional)
- 1/4 cup cilantro leaves, chopped (or parsley)
- salt, to taste

Jamaican-Style Dumplings

- 1/2 cup gluten-free flour

- 1/4 cup water
- Pinch of salt

Instructions

- Plug in your Instant Pot and press saute mode button. Add oil, once heated add dry spices, curry powder, paprika, cumin, turmeric, thyme and cook for a minute stirring constantly.
- Add onion, garlic, ginger, spring onion and cook until for 2 minutes or until onions are soft. Add jackfruit, potato, carrots and stir to coat.
- Add coconut milk, vegetable broth or bouillon plus water, Italian seasoning, cayenne pepper, and dumplings stir.
- Close Instant Pot lid and press manual mode for 10 minutes. When finished, allow Instant Pot to natural release for 10 minutes. Carefully release the knob to release the remaining pressure. Remove lid, stir in cilantro leaves, crush some of the potatoes to thicken curry and check seasonings.

Jamaican Style Dumplings

- To prepare dumplings, combine flour and salt in a medium bowl, add water and mix to combine.
- Knead dough to form a smooth ball. Take small pieces of dough and roll between palms of your hand to form cylindrical shapes or balls and drop on top of the curry.

Chicken Rice and Peas

Ingredients

- 12 chicken thighs, bone in
- 1 lime, halved
- hot sauce, to serve (optional)
- For the marinade
- 1 big bunch spring onions, roughly chopped
- thumb-sized piece ginger, roughly chopped
- 3 garlic cloves
- ½ a small onion
- 3 scotch bonnet chilies
- ½ tsp dried thyme, or 1 tbsp thyme leaves
- 1 lime, juiced
- 2 tbsp soy sauce
- 2 tbsp vegetable oil
- 3 tbsp brown sugar
- 1 tbsp ground allspice
- For the rice & peas
- 200g basmati rice
- 400g can coconut milk
- 1 bunch spring onions, sliced
- 2 large thyme sprigs
- 2 garlic cloves, finely chopped
- 1 tsp ground allspice
- 2 x 410g cans kidney beans, drained

Instructions

- For the marinade, combine the spring onions, ginger, garlic, onion, scotch bonnet chillies, dried thyme, lime juice, soy sauce, vegetable oil, brown sugar and ground allspice in a food processor along with 1 tsp salt, and blend to a purée.
- Make a few slashes in 12 chicken thighs and pour the marinade over the meat, rubbing it into all the crevices.
- Cover and leave to marinate overnight in the fridge.
- To cook in the oven, heat to 180C/160C fan/gas 4. Put the chicken pieces in a roasting tin with the halved lime and cook for 45 mins until tender and cooked through.
- While the chicken is cooking, prepare the rice & peas. Rinse the basmati rice in plenty of cold water, then tip it into a large saucepan. Add the coconut milk, spring onions, thyme sprigs, garlic and ground allspice.
- Season with salt, add 300ml cold water and set over a high heat. Once the rice begins to boil, turn it down to a medium heat, cover and cook for 10 mins.
- Add the kidney beans to the rice, then cover with a lid. Leave off the heat for 5 mins until all the liquid is absorbed.
- Squeeze the roasted lime over the chicken and serve with the rice & peas, and some hot sauce if you like it really spicy.

Caribbean Banana Curry Bake

Ingredients

- 1 onion sliced
- 2 cloves garlic chopped
- 1 inch chunk ginger
- 1 red pepper
- 1/2 medium butternut squash
- 2 medium potatoes
- 1 tbsp jerk seasoning
- 1 tbsp sunflower or vegetable oil
- 400 g tinned coconut milk
- 2 bananas sliced
- 400 g tinned chickpeas drained and rinsed
- small handful fresh coriander roughly chopped

Instructions

- Preheat the oven to 200°C (fan)/220°C/gas mark 7
- Get a large roasting tin ready.
- Peel and slice an onion and place in the roasting tin. Chop two cloves of garlic, peel and chop a 1 inch piece of ginger and add those to the tin.
- Deseed and chop a red pepper and 1/2 butternut squash (no need to peel as long as it's washed). Add to your roasting tin.
- Chop two medium potatoes into bite-sized pieces and add to the tin.
- Sprinkle over 1 tbsp jerk seasoning and 1 tbsp sunflower oil. Mix well with a spoon ensuring that everything is well coated.
- Roast for 45 minutes. Stir two or three times to ensure that the potatoes don't stick.
- Once the vegetables are almost done slice two bananas and add them to your roasting dish along with a tin of coconut milk and a drained tin of chickpeas.
- Return to the oven for 5-10 minutes to warm through. Don't overcook the bananas.
- Sprinkle over the coriander.
- Serve with a cabbage based salad and rice.

Vegan Paella

Ingredients

- 200 g 1 cup of brown short grain bomba rice
- 1 small yellow bell pepper sliced
- 1 small red bell pepper sliced
- 2 1/2 cups of vegetable stock
- 200 g 1 cup sweet green peas
- 1/2 tsp of saffron threads
- 4 to 5 sprigs of thyme stems removed
- 1 red onion sliced
- 2 scallion chopped
- 100 g of mushrooms sliced
- 200 g 1 cup pumpkin, cubed & peeled
- 200 g 1 cup sweet potato, cubed & peeled
- 4 pimento seeds 1/4 tsp allspice
- 1 cinnamon stick
- 1/2 tsp black pepper
- 3 garlic cloves minced

- 1/4 tsp of paprika smoked or regular
- 1 bay leaf
- 1 scotch bonnet whole
- himalayan pink salt according to taste
- 1 lime
- *coconut oil

Instructions

- Combine the vegetable stock with the saffron threads, bring to the boil then reduce to a simmer for 5 minutes and set aside.
- Meanwhile heat your paella pan with 2 tablespoons of coconut oil then temper the cinnamon stick and pimento (allspice) until the aroma is released, once an aroma is achieved add the bay leaf and continue to temper for another 30 seconds before sauteing the garlic, scallion and red onions for 2 minutes.
- Proceed to add the bell peppers then cook until softened, this should take 3-5 minutes in total.
- Fold the pumpkin, mushrooms and sweet potatoes pieces into the pan, don't forget to maneuver/rotate the pan during cooking.
- Season the entire pan with the thyme, black pepper and your desired amount of pink salt - 1 teaspoon worth was suffice for me.

- Add the bomba rice along with the paprika, use a wooden spoon to fully coat/combine the bomba rice with the seasoning and mix through.
- Gradually add the saffron infused stock to the paella.
- Then add the remaining stock to the pan and leave uncovered for 5 minutes.
- Finally sprinkle the green peas along with the scotch bonnet to the pan before covering with foil to steam for 10 minutes.
- After 10 minutes turn off the heat and leave to settle for 5 minutes before removing the foil to serve.
- Don't forgot to squeeze some lime over the top and garnish with further thyme

Vegan Caribbean Bowl

Ingredients

Marinade

- 1/2 cup fresh squeezed orange juice
- 1/4 cup soy sauce
- 1 Tablespoon jerk seasoning
- 1 teaspoon toasted sesame oil (Asian variety)
- 12 ounces tempeh, or other protein (pork chicken, shrimp)

Rice

- 1 cup jasmine rice
- 1 cup coconut milk
- 1 cup broth
- 1 tsp salt
- 1/4 cup shredded, unsweetened dried coconut flakes

Vegetables

- 4 leaves kale or collard greens, destemmed
- 1/4 white cabbage
- 1/2 red bell pepper
- 1 lime, halved horizontally

Assembly

- 1 Tablespoon coconut oil
- 1/2 orange
- 1-2 teaspoon/s sesame oil, optional

Garnish

- Sliced avocado, lime, orange, pineapple, and/or grated carrot and minced scallion and cilantro to taste, in any combination

Instructions

Marinade

Mix all ingredients together. Halve tempeh down center, then cube. If using other protein, cut in uniform slices or cubes. Add protein to marinade and let soak for a minimum of 30 minutes.

Rice

While protein marinades, begin rice. Add liquids, rice, coconut, and salt to medium saucepan. Bring to a boil over medium high heat. Reduce heat to simmer/medium low, and cover for 20 minutes. Turn of heat and let rice stand.

Vegetables

While rice cooks, slice collards or kale very thin. Separately, slice thin or shred cabbage, and julienne red pepper. Place cabbage and red pepper in a bowl; squeeze on half a lime. Thinly slice remaining lime for garnish if desired.

Assembly

- Heat pan over medium high heat, then add coconut oil. Remove tempeh or other protein from marinade and place in hot oil, browning well on each side. If you feel you need more oil, drizzle in another teaspoon or so of sesame oil. Squeeze in half an orange.
- Remove tempeh from pan. Add dark greens, and pour in marinade. Sauté over low heat until desired doneness, approximately 10 minutes. Place rice, protein, raw veggies, cooked veggies, and garnish on the plate or in the bowl as you like. Add desired garnishes.

Jamaican Jerk Seasoning

Ingredients

- 25-30 green onions
- 1 thick 3 ½ x 1-inch piece of fresh ginger
- 1 or 2 Scotch bonnet or habanero peppers
- 5 garlic cloves
- 2 tablespoons fresh thyme leaves
- ½ cup canola oil or another neutral-flavored oil
- ½ cup soy sauce
- ½ cup tomato sauce
- 1/3 cup fresh orange juice
- 1/3 cup distilled white vinegar
- 3 tablespoons fresh lime juice
- 3 tablespoons brown sugar
- 1 tablespoon plus 1 ½ teaspoons pink or sea salt
- 1 tablespoon plus 1 ½ teaspoons ground cloves
- 1 tablespoon plus 1 ½ teaspoons ground allspice
- 1 ½ teaspoons ground nutmeg
- ¼ to ½ teaspoon ground cinnamon or cassia

Instructions

- Put the green onions, ginger, Scotch bonnets, garlic, and thyme in a food processor and process for 30 seconds.

- Add the oil, soy sauce, tomato sauce, orange juice, vinegar, lime juice, brown sugar, salt, cloves, allspice, nutmeg, and cinnamon and process until medium smooth.
- Transfer to a clean jar, seal, and refrigerate.

Classic Barbadian Sweet Potato Pie

Ingredients

- 1 pound, 6 ounces white- or yellow-fleshed sweet potatoes, coarsely chopped
- 2 tablespoons vegan margarine
- ½ cup pineapple juice
- 1 teaspoon ground cinnamon or cassia
- Pink or sea salt
- 2 pineapple slices
- 2 cherries
- 2 teaspoons granulated sugar

Instructions

- Cook the sweet potatoes in boiling salted water until tender.
- Preheat the oven to 350°F. Grease two 8-ounce ramekins.
- Drain the sweet potatoes, add the margarine, pineapple juice, and cinnamon, and mash until smooth. Season with salt to taste.
- Transfer to the prepared ramekins. Top each pie with a pineapple slice and a cherry and sprinkle with sugar. Broil for about 5 minutes, until lightly browned. Serve warm.

Onion Gravy

Ingredients

- 1 tablespoon vegan margarine or olive oil
- 1 medium-large onion, thinly sliced
- 1 tomato, thinly sliced
- 2 garlic cloves, pressed
- 1 teaspoon fresh marjoram minced
- 1 teaspoon fresh thyme minced
- 1 teaspoon onion powder
- 1 teaspoon adobo seasoning
- ¼ teaspoon mild paprika
- 1 cup water
- 2 tablespoons ketchup
- 1 teaspoon soy sauce
- ¼ teaspoon Caribbean Caramel (optional)
- ¼ teaspoon cornstarch
- ½ teaspoon American-style prepared mustard

Instructions

- Heat the margarine in a skillet over medium heat.
- Add the onion, tomato, and garlic and sauté for 3 to 5 minutes, until the onion is slightly tender.

- Add the marjoram, thyme, onion powder, adobo seasoning, and paprika, then stir in the water. Cook for another 5 minutes, then stir in the ketchup, soy sauce, Caribbean Caramel, cornstarch mixed with 1 tablespoon of water, and the mustard.
- Simmer, stirring occasionally, for about 15 minutes, until the sauce starts to get slightly thick.

Black Cake (Rum)

- ¼ cup plus 2 tablespoons dark rum
- ¼ cup white rum, or additional dark rum
- 2 tablespoons falernum
- ½ cup raisins
- ½ cup vegan margarine
- ½ cup vegetable shortening
- 1 cup light brown sugar
- 2 tablespoons warm water
- 1 teaspoon vanilla essence, or ½ teaspoon vanilla extract
- 2 cups unbleached all-purpose flour
- 1 teaspoon ground cinnamon
- ½ teaspoon pink or sea salt
- ½ teaspoon baking powder
- ½ teaspoon baking soda
- 1 teaspoon apple cider vinegar
- 1 cup nondairy milk
- 1 tablespoon molasses

Rum Glaze

- ¼ cup vegan margarine
- ¼ cup water
- 3 tablespoon brown sugar
- 1 teaspoon vanilla essence, or ½ teaspoon vanilla extract
- ¼ cup dark rum

Instructions

- To make the cake, pour ¼ cup of the dark rum, the white rum, and the falernum over the raisins and let them soak overnight in a covered container.
- Preheat the oven to 350°F.
- Cream the margarine and shortening with the sugar until fluffy using an electric mixer. Whisk the water and egg replacer together, then add to the sugar mixture, along with the vanilla essence. Stir until evenly incorporated. Add the flour, cinnamon, salt, baking powder, and baking soda and mix until just incorporated.
- Stir the vinegar into the milk, then mix into the batter. Fold in the raisins and their liquid, the molasses, and the remaining 2 tablespoons of dark rum.
- Scrape the batter into the prepared pan and bake for 35 to 40 minutes, until brown and the top of the cake springs back when gently pressed.

- Meanwhile, make the glaze. Combine the margarine, water, brown sugar, and vanilla essence in a small saucepan over low heat. Cook, stirring frequently, until the sugar has dissolved. Turn off the heat and stir in the rum. 7 Glaze the cake as it cools. Let cool completely before serving.

Vegan Curry

Ingredients

- Chickpeas (1 can)
- Chopped tomatoes (1 can or fresh equivalent)
- Scotch bonnet tops (or two tablespoons of scotch bonnet hot sauce)
- One large potato
- 1 spring onion
- Half an onion
- 3 garlic cloves
- 1 lime
- Spinach (half a packet)
- Hot curry powder or mild curry powder
- Jamaican curry power
- All purpose seasoning
- Thyme
- Black pepper
- Soy sauce

Instructions

- Sweat your diced onion and chopped garlic in a frying pan in a tablespoon of oil on a low heat.
- Add your cubes potatoes and fry until translucent.
- Add your spring onion and chopped tomatoes. Turn this onto a high heat until the mixture bubbles then turn down to a low heat.
- Add the curry powders, all purpose, black pepper, thyme, soy sauce and whole scotch bonnet. Bring this to a high heat also for a few minutes then turn down to low and remove the scotch bonnets.
- Add your chickpeas and cook for a further 10-15 minutes on a low heat.
- Add your spinach and squeeze half a lime through the curry.
- Serve with rice, fried plantain and naan bread.

Veggie Bowl

Ingredients

Cauliflower Rice and Peas

- 1 head of cauliflower
- 1 teaspoon olive oil
- ½ onion, finely chopped
- 1 clove garlic, minced
- 1 teaspoon dried thyme
- 1 can (15 ounces) of kidney beans, drained
- ¼ cup canned coconut milk

Veggies

- 2 red peppers, chopped into chunks
- 1 large sweet potato, peeled and chopped into coins
- 1 unripe (green) plantain, chopped in to coins
- 2 zucchinis, chopped
- 1 onion, roughly chopped into wedges
- 1 tablespoon olive oil
- Vegetable seasoning (optional)
- ½ teaspoon ground allspice
- ½ teaspoon dried thyme
- Salt and pepper

Mango Habanero Vinaigrette

- 1 mango, peeled and roughly chopped
- ¼ small habanero pepper, roughly chopped
- 1 clove of garlic, roughly chopped
- 1 tablespoon red wine vinegar
- 1 teaspoon Dijon mustard
- 1 teaspoon olive oil

Optional

- Chopped fresh cilantro

Instructions

Cauliflower Rice and Peas

- Chop the cauliflower into large florets.
- Place ⅓ of the florets into a food processor. Give it a few quick pulses and then process for about 10 seconds until the cauliflower resembles rice kernels.
- Transfer the cauliflower rice to a large bowl.
- Repeat this process 2 more times with the remaining florets.
- In a large sauté pan, heat 1 tsp of olive oil over medium heat.
- Once heated, add the chopped onion and sprinkle with salt. Cook the onion for about 2 minutes.

- Add in the garlic and dried thyme and cook for 1 minute.
- Add the kidney beans to the pan and sprinkle with salt. Stir to incorporate and cook for another minute.
- Add in the coconut milk and cauliflower rice and sprinkle with salt. Cook for 4-5 minutes, stirring occasionally, until the cauliflower rice is slightly tender.
- Take the rice and peas off the heat and set aside.
- Give the rice and peas a taste and add salt and pepper if needed.

Grilled veggies

- Place the chopped vegetables in a large bowl or on a large baking sheet.
- Drizzle the veggies with olive oil and add in the vegetable seasoning, all spice, thyme, and a healthy sprinkle of salt and pepper.
- Toss the vegetables to coat all the pieces with the oil and seasoning.
- Heat a grill pan on the stove over medium-high heat. Or, fire up the barbecue grill to medium heat.
- Working in batches, cook the veggies until they are tender and have a nice char on the outside. Cooking time will vary depending on the vegetable. Sweet potatoes and plantains will need to cook about 7 minutes on each side, red pepper 5-6 minutes on each side, and zucchini and onions 3-4 minutes on each side.

Mango Habanero Vinaigrette

- While the veggies are cooking, place all vinaigrette ingredients into a food processor, blender, or nutribullet.
- Blend until the mixture reaches a smooth consistency.
- Assemble the bowls: Place about 1 ½ cups of cauliflower rice and peas into each bowl.
- Top the rice and peas with about 2 cups of mixed veggies. Or, divide each type of veggie into quarters and evenly distribute among the 4 bowls.
- Drizzle the veggies with 3 tablespoons of vinaigrette and sprinkle with fresh cilantro if desired.

Caribbean Tofu

Ingredients

For the tofu:

- 800g extra firm tofu; drained, pressed for at least 30 minutes, and cut into cubes
- 2tbsp olive oil for cooking

For the marinade:

- 2tsp ground coriander
- 1tsp turmeric
- 1tsp ground all spice
- 1-2tsp chili flakes
- 1tsp black pepper
- Juice of 2 limes

For the quinoa:

- 200g quinoa, well rinsed
- 350ml water
- 2tbsp desiccated coconut

Instructions

- In a large bowl, mix all of the marinade ingredients together until they form a smooth liquid.
- Add the cubes of tofu to the bowl and coat thoroughly in the marinade. Set aside.
- In a large pan, bring the water to the boil. Once boiling add the rinsed quinoa, stir once, and simmer for ten minutes. At the this point, add the desiccated coconut, stir well and simmer for a further five to six minutes. If at any point it begins sticking to the pan, add a little extra water.
- After adding the coconut to the quinoa, heat the olive oil in a frying pan over a medium-high heat.
- Once the oil is hot, carefully place the cubes of marinated tofu into the frying pan. Fry for around five minutes, turning frequently, until it has browned on all sides.
- Remove from the heat and use kitchen paper to remove any excess oil.
- Remove the quinoa from the heat, set aside for two minutes, then fluff up with fork.
- Serve as it is or with a sauce of your choice.

Smoothie

Ingredients

- 1 x banana
- 1 x mango
- 1 x pear (optional)
- Coconut milk
- 1 tablespoon of chia seeds

Instructions

- Put all the ingredients into a blender
- Blend

Jerk Cauliflower

Ingredients

- Half a head of cauliflower, broken it to bite size florets
- 1 – 2 Tbsp Jerk seasoning
- 2 Tbsp oil
- Spring onions, finely chopped.
- Vegan mayonnaise
- Chives to serve

Instructions

- Put the florets in a bowl with the oil and then Spread out on a baking tray and put in an oven at 180c for 20 mins. They should soften and brown slightly.
- Carefully transfer the cauliflower to a bowl and add as much jerk seasoning as it takes to give your cauliflower a good coating.
- Put the cauliflower back on the baking tray and give it another 10 mins in the oven. I like my cauliflower quite well cooked and soft all the way through. Some people prefer cauliflower with more bite, in which case reduce your cooking times accordingly.

- Once nicely soft and browned, transfer to serving dish, top with Spring onions and a drizzle of vegan mayo and you're done.

Sweet Potato and Ginger

Ingredients

- 750g Sweet potato
- 30g Fresh root ginger
- Olive Oil
- Salt and Pepper

Instructions

Wash the sweet potatoes and bake them in the oven until soft.
Grate the ginger and gently fry in some olive oil.
Once the potatoes have cooked, peel and put the flesh into a mixing bowl.
Using a mixer, either free standing or hand held, beat the sweet potato along with the ginger, salt and pepper until you have a smooth consistency.

Caribbean Yellow Rice Medley

Ingredients

- 1 tablespoon organic coconut oil
- 1 medium onion, chopped
- 2-3 garlic cloves, minced or pressed
- ½ green pepper, chopped
- ½ red pepper, chopped
- 1 10-ounce can organic diced tomatoes and green chilies
- 4 medium organic sweet potatoes, peeled and cut into cite-sized pieces
- 2 19-ounce cans organic cannellini beans, including the liquid
- 1 teaspoon grated organic ginger
- 1 teaspoon dark brown sugar
- ½ teaspoon organic allspice
- 12 teaspoon organic ground cumin
- 3 bay leaves
- ½ cup organic vegetable stock
- Sea salt and freshly ground black pepper
- 1 12-ounce package Chicken Tenders, frozen
- 2 cups organic spinach leaves, sliced into thin slivers
- 1 tablespoon organic coconut oil
- ½ medium onion, chopped
- 2 cloves garlic, minced
- 1 teaspoon turmeric
- 1½ cup organic jasmine rice

- 2¾ - 3 cups boiling water
- ½ teaspoon sea salt
- 1 cup frozen organic green peas

Instructions

- Heat a large skillet and add the coconut oil. Add the onions and cook for 4-5 minutes. Add the garlic and chopped peppers.
- Transfer to slow cooker if you were using a skillet. Add the tomatoes and chills, sweet potatoes, beans, ginger, brown sugar, allspice, cumin, bay leaves, stock, sea salt and pepper.
- Cover and cook 4 hours on high or 6 hours on low.
- Add the Chicken Tenders and the slivered spinach. Taste and adjust seasonings. Remove the bay leaves and serve with Caribbean Yellow Rice.
- To make the Caribbean Yellow Rice, heat a 3 quart saucepan, and melt the coconut oil.
- Sauté the onion until translucent, add the garlic, and then turmeric.
- Add the rice and sauté for 2 minutes. Make sure the rice is uniformly yellow.
- Add the boiling water and sea salt. Cover and cook for 10 minutes.
- Add the frozen green peas and cook 6-8 more minutes.

Vegan Caribbean Stew

Ingredients

- 1 cup uncooked brown rice
- 2 cups water
- ½ pound collard greens, chopped
- 2 cloves garlic, peeled
- 1 (10 ounce) package frozen okra
- 1 (28 ounce) can whole peeled tomatoes, chopped, with liquid
- 1 chayote squash, diced
- 2 cloves garlic, crushed
- ¼ teaspoon ground ginger, or more to taste
- ¼ teaspoon dried dill weed, or more to taste
- ¼ teaspoon ground cumin, or to taste
- 1 tablespoon chopped fresh cilantro, or to taste
- 1 (16 ounce) can kidney beans, rinsed and drained
- 1 (6 ounce) can tomato paste
- 1 teaspoon all-purpose flour,

Instructions

- Bring brown rice and water to a boil in a saucepan over high heat. Reduce heat to medium-low; cover and simmer until rice is tender and the liquid has been absorbed, 45 to 50 minutes.
- Place collard greens and 2 peeled whole garlic cloves in a pot; add enough water to cover. Boil until collards are tender, about 15 minutes. Drain.
- Combine okra, tomatoes, chayote squash, and 2 crushed garlic cloves in a separate large pot; bring to a boil and cook until okra has thawed, about 5 minutes. Reduce to a simmer; season with ground ginger, dill weed, ground cumin, and cilantro to taste. Add collard greens; simmer until flavors have blended, at least 40 minutes (1 hour for best flavor).
- Mash kidney beans together with tomato paste in a bowl; add to the stew. Stir in cooked rice and mix well. Add a spoonful of flour to thicken, if desired. Adjust seasonings to taste.

Jerk Chili

Ingredients

- 2 tablespoons olive oil
- 3 cloves garlic, finely chopped
- 2 celery stalks, diced
- 1 onion, diced
- 1 red bell pepper, diced
- 2 teaspoons Jamaican jerk seasoning or chili sauce
- 1 cup coconut milk
- 3 tablespoons tomato purée (passata)
- 1 cup canned red or kidney beans, drained
- 2 tablespoons fresh lime juice
- 1 mango, diced
- 1/2 cup chopped cilantro (coriander)
- Cooked basmati rice, to serve

Instructions

- Heat the olive oil in a large saucepan over medium heat. Add the garlic, celery, onion, and bell pepper and sauté for 5-6 minutes, until the onion is translucent. Add the jerk seasoning or chili sauce and cook for 2-3 minutes.

- Stir in the coconut milk, tomato purée, beans, and fresh lime juice and season to taste with salt and freshly ground black pepper, if needed. Cover the saucepan with a lid, reduce the heat to low, and simmer for 20 minutes, stirring occasionally.
- Stir in half of the mango and half of the cilantro, then cover the saucepan and simmer for another 10 minutes. Serve the chili over rice, garnished with the remaining mango and cilantro.

Caribbean Cauliflower Curry

Ingredients

For the curry spice mix

- 2 tbsp Curry
- 2 tsp Turmeric
- 1/2 tbsp Paprika
- 1 tsp Cumin
- 1 tsp Coriander optional
- 2 tsp Salt
- 2 tsp Pepper

For the cauliflower

- 1 tbsp coconut oil olive or canola are fine too
- 1 medium onion chopped
- 4 garlic cloves minced
- 1 tbsp fresh ginger minced

- 1 whole habanero punctured on all sides with a sharp knife
- 15 oz can diced tomatoes fire roasted
- 15 oz can coconut milk
- 3 thyme sprigs
- 1 bay leaf
- 1 medium cauliflower chopped into small florets
- 1 small lime for zest

Instructions

Make the Curry Spice Mix

Mix all ingredients in a mixing bowl and set aside

Make the Cauliflower

- Heat skillet on medium-high heat and add coconut oil.
- Sauté onions for 2-3 minutes until they brown a little and become translucent.
- Add the garlic and ginger with a 1/3 the spice mix. Mix well and sauce 30-60 seconds.

- Add the habanero, then the thyme, bay leaf and tomatoes with their juices. Add another 1/3 spice mix and mix well. Cook about 2-3 minutes to reduce the juices from the tomatoes.
- Add coconut milk. Let cook 2-3 minutes.
- Add cauliflower and let simmer until preferred tenderness 15-20 minutes. Start using the fork test after about 10 minutes of cooking. Add the remaining spice mix about halfway.
- Finish the cauliflower by grating some of the zest into the finished dish.
- Serve over rice with fresh parsley or cilantro and some lime juice.

mindplusfood

FREE BONUS

Thank you for your purchase. Subscribe
to mindplusfood.com for a free 41-Page
holistic health and weight loss cheat
sheet and exclusive wellness content

HOLISTIC WEIGHT
LOSS AND HEALTH